Growth Mindset Journal

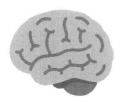

For girls

Anything is possible
with the right mindset

If you can dream it and believe it, you can achieve anything. This journal is dedicated to those who are ready to build a mindset that sets them up for success no matter the circumstance.

Use this guided journal to plan your best life. Create a morning and night time routine that helps you live life to the fullest. Learn new ways to manage stress, friendships and relationships. Tackle life's challenges and have a lot of fun along the way.

Share these exercises with your best friends or family.

The words we use:

Fixed Mindset

I'm not good at this

I give up

I'm never going to get this.

I hate making mistakes.

Growth Mindset

I'll try another approach

I'll keep trying

I've got this.

Mistakes help me learn.

Change your words and you'll change your mindset

Date: ____/____/_____

I believe I can do anything I put my mind to because...

_____

_____

_____

_____

_____

_____

If I knew I wouldn't fail, I would...

_____

_____

_____

_____

_____

_____

Date: ____/____/_____

These are the subjects I'm great at...

_____

_____

_____

_____

_____

_____

_____

These are the subjects I could spend more time on...

_____

_____

_____

_____

_____

_____

Date: ____/____/_____

My proudest moment is...

_____

_____

_____

_____

_____

_____

_____

_____

_____

_____

_____

_____

_____

_____

_____

_____

Date: ____/____/_____

The last mistake I made was...

_____

_____

_____

_____

_____

_____

_____

This is what I've learned from that mistake...

_____

_____

_____

_____

_____

_____

Transform your thinking to transform your grades.

A simple shift in thinking could turn your grades from good to great. Fill in the blanks.

i.e. I don't understand this.

i.e. I may not understand this now but I'll find ways to figure it out

I'm either good at something or I'm not.

She's just smarter than I am.

This task is impossible.

I won't be able to figure this out.

Date: ___/___/_____

What will you do to challenge yourself today?

_____

_____

_____

_____

_____

_____

_____

What's the last challenge you had to overcome?

_____

_____

_____

_____

_____

_____

_____

Date: ____/____/_____

Fill in the blank. I don't feel great about myself when...

_____

_____

_____

_____

_____

_____

What can you do to change how you feel when things
don't go your way?

_____

_____

_____

_____

_____

Date: ____/____/_____

When someone criticises me I feel...

_____

_____

_____

_____

_____

_____

_____

What can I use criticism and feedback to improve
instead?

_____

_____

_____

_____

_____

_____

Date: ____/____/_____

My closest friends are...

_____

_____

_____

_____

_____

_____

_____

This is what I can do to be a better friend for them...

_____

_____

_____

_____

_____

Date: ___ / ___ / _____

When my friends and I disagree with something I...

_____

_____

_____

_____

_____

_____

_____

This is how I could handle it better...

_____

_____

_____

_____

_____

_____

Date: ____/____/_____

My siblings/family and I have disagreements when...

_____

_____

_____

_____

_____

_____

_____

This is how I could handle it better...

_____

_____

_____

_____

_____

You are enough.

Date: ___ / ___ / _____

If you could live out your wildest dreams tomorrow,
what would your day look like? (Don't hold back)

_____

_____

_____

_____

_____

_____

_____

_____

_____

_____

_____

_____

Date: ____/____/_____

Aside from the teachers at school, who do you learn from?

_____

_____

_____

_____

_____

_____

Is there anyone else (you haven't met) that you'd like to learn from?

_____

_____

_____

_____

_____

_____

_____

Date: ___ / ___ / _____

What did you do today that made you think hard?

_____

_____

_____

_____

_____

_____

_____

_____

_____

_____

_____

_____

_____

_____

Transform your thinking to transform your life.

A simple shift in thinking could turn your grades around.
Fill in the blanks.

Instead of...	Try thinking...
I don't like the way I look.	I look beautiful and healthy.
I'm a loner.	I have lots of friends who love me.
People are always judging me.	
I need to lose more weight.	
Other people are so much prettier than I am.	
My nose is too big.	
Plastic surgery will fix me.	

You are capable of much more than you think.

Date: ____/____/_____

Think of a time when you were very upset. What caused it?

_____
_____
_____
_____
_____
_____
_____

How did you deal with it?

_____
_____
_____
_____
_____
_____
_____

Using meditation to cope when going gets rough

No matter how much we plan, life is going to throw us some curve balls. You can't predict what will happen tomorrow but you can find ways to cope with difficult situations using meditation.

Meditation calms your mind, helps improve your focus and it lifts your mood regardless of the day you've had.

Try it: Find a quiet corner in your room and plant yourself on a comfortable chair. Close your eyes and breathe in and out slowly.

Focus on being present.

This can be hard at first but with practice you'll start to see the benefits of taking quiet time out everyday.

DOODLES

You can be anyone and do anything if you put your mind to it.
With this in mind, draw your dream life.

Your morning routine

Having a consistent morning routine can help you prepare for a big day ahead. It can help you focus, get organised, clear your mind and relax for what may be a stressful day.

An example of a morning routine could consist of some light stretches and breakfast followed by a mini meditation or a dance off with your brother and sister.

Your morning routine

1.
2.
3.
4.
5.

Date: ____/____/_____

When was the last time you disagreed with someone?
How did you handle the conflict?

_____

_____

_____

_____

_____

_____

_____

_____

_____

_____

_____

_____

_____

Your night time routine

A night time routine can help you get a good night's rest and get your organised for the next day.

It can be the difference between a good and a great night's sleep. Aim to shut off all electronic devices at least two hours before going to bed. Use the time to layout your clothes for the next day or read a book.

An example of a night time routine could consist of yoga, reading a book and laying out your clothes.

Your night time routine

1.
2.
3.
4.
5.

Date: ___/___/_____

Write about a challenge you've had this year.

_____

_____

_____

_____

_____

_____

_____

How did you overcome it?

_____

_____

_____

_____

_____

_____

The prettiest people are always the happiest.

Date: ___/___/_____

Everyone has a different definition of success. What
does success mean to you?

_____

_____

_____

_____

_____

_____

_____

_____

_____

_____

_____

_____

_____

Date: ___/___/_____

What are some things you'd like to do but are afraid to?

_____

_____

_____

_____

_____

_____

_____

_____

_____

_____

_____

_____

_____

Date: ___/___/_____

When was the last time you tried/learned something
new? Write about the experience.

_____

_____

_____

_____

_____

_____

_____

_____

_____

_____

_____

_____

_____

_____

The quickest way to learn
is to fail fast.

The bucket list

Write down a list of everything you want to learn/do.
Don't hold back!

The travel list

Write down a list of all the places you want to go. I.e. See the snow monkeys in Japan.

People to meet

Write down a list of all the people you want to meet.

Anything is possible.

Your vision board

If you can dream it, you can make it your reality.
Take your bucket list, travel like, people you'd like to meet list and put it into a vision board or draw it here. Share it with your family.

Date: ____/____/_____

Write down a challenge that's taught you a lesson you wouldn't learn in school.

_____

_____

_____

_____

_____

_____

_____

_____

_____

_____

_____

_____

_____

Date: ____/____/_____

Think of one thing you'd like to change in the world.
How can you help?

_____

_____

_____

_____

_____

_____

_____

_____

_____

_____

_____

_____

_____

You've got this!

Word Power

Our words create our reality. They drive how we see the world. It's easy to use strong, positive words when life is going great. However, it's a bit harder to do when challenge arises.

This is where the power of affirmations comes in. Affirmations are a set of words you can use to lift your spirit and mindset when you've had a bad day at school, got into an argument with a friend or maybe even some critical feedback from your teacher(s).

Try this: Write some affirmations of your own. Here are a few examples you can use: I am awesome!, I trust myself, I am worthy, I accept myself.

Date: ____/____/_____

Journal about a time when you solved a problem you
thought was impossible.

_____

_____

_____

_____

_____

_____

_____

What steps did you take to solve the problem?

_____

_____

_____

_____

_____

Draw this

What do you think the world will be like 10 years from now?
Draw it.

You are worthy.

Celebrating the small wins!

When we place too much focus on our challenges and failures, we lose sight of all our 'wins', all the little challenges we overcome. The following pages are to help document all your wins!

This could be acing a difficult test, making it through gym class or helping a friend finish her science project.

Write it all down!

Date: ____/____/_____

When I come across a new problem I tend to...

_____

_____

_____

_____

_____

_____

Ways I can cope better with new problems...

_____

_____

_____

_____

_____

_____

Date: ____/____/_____

What will a successful year at school look like? i.e.
Good grades, a close group of friends, making it onto
a sports team...

_____

_____

_____

_____

_____

_____

_____

_____

_____

_____

_____

_____

Date: ___/___/_____

People who inspire me to keep learning are...

Daily Journal Prompts

Date: ___/___/_____

A challenge I came across...

_____

_____

_____

_____

_____

_____

_____

How I overcame it...

_____

_____

_____

_____

_____

_____

Date: ____/____/_____

A challenge I came across...

_____

_____

_____

_____

_____

_____

_____

_____

How I overcame it...

_____

_____

_____

_____

_____

_____

_____

Date: ____/____/_____

A challenge I came across...

_____

_____

_____

_____

_____

_____

_____

How I overcame it...

_____

_____

_____

_____

_____

_____

_____

Date: ____/____/_____

A challenge I came across...

_____
_____
_____
_____
_____
_____
_____

How I overcame it...

_____
_____
_____
_____
_____
_____

Date: ____/____/_____

A challenge I came across...

_____

_____

_____

_____

_____

_____

_____

How I overcame it...

_____

_____

_____

_____

_____

_____

Date: ____/____/_____

A challenge I came across...

_____

_____

_____

_____

_____

_____

_____

How I overcame it...

_____

_____

_____

_____

_____

_____

_____

Date: ____/____/_____

A challenge I came across...

_____

_____

_____

_____

_____

_____

_____

How I overcame it...

_____

_____

_____

_____

_____

_____

_____

Date: ____/____/_____

A challenge I came across...

_____

_____

_____

_____

_____

_____

_____

How I overcame it...

_____

_____

_____

_____

_____

_____

_____

Date: ___ / ___ / _____

A challenge I came across...

_____

_____

_____

_____

_____

_____

_____

_____

How I overcame it...

_____

_____

_____

_____

_____

_____

_____

Date: ____/____/_____

A challenge I came across...

_____

_____

_____

_____

_____

_____

_____

_____

How I overcame it...

_____

_____

_____

_____

_____

_____

Date: ____/____/_____

A challenge I came across...

_____

_____

_____

_____

_____

_____

_____

How I overcame it...

_____

_____

_____

_____

_____

_____

_____

Date: ____/____/_____

A challenge I came across...

_____

_____

_____

_____

_____

_____

_____

How I overcame it...

_____

_____

_____

_____

_____

_____

_____

Date: ____/____/_____

A challenge I came across...

_____

_____

_____

_____

_____

_____

_____

How I overcame it...

_____

_____

_____

_____

_____

_____

_____

Date: ____/____/_____

A challenge I came across...

_____

_____

_____

_____

_____

_____

_____

How I overcame it...

_____

_____

_____

_____

_____

_____

Date: ____/____/_____

A challenge I came across...

_____

_____

_____

_____

_____

_____

_____

How I overcame it...

_____

_____

_____

_____

_____

_____

Date: ____/ ____/ _____

A challenge I came across...

_____

_____

_____

_____

_____

_____

_____

How I overcame it...

_____

_____

_____

_____

_____

_____

Date: ____/____/_____

A challenge I came across...

_____

_____

_____

_____

_____

_____

_____

How I overcame it...

_____

_____

_____

_____

_____

_____

Kicking goals

A goal without a plan is just a wish. Use the following goal planners to map out exactly how you'll achieve your goals.

Remember, no goal is ever too big.

Weekly goals

SUNDAY

MONDAY

TUESDAY

WEDNESDAY

THURSDAY

FRIDAY

SATURDAY

Weekly goals

SUNDAY

MONDAY

TUESDAY

WEDNESDAY

THURSDAY

FRIDAY

SATURDAY

Weekly goals

SUNDAY

MONDAY

TUESDAY

WEDNESDAY

THURSDAY

FRIDAY

SATURDAY

Weekly goals

SUNDAY

MONDAY

TUESDAY

WEDNESDAY

THURSDAY

FRIDAY

SATURDAY

Weekly goals

SUNDAY

MONDAY

TUESDAY

WEDNESDAY

THURSDAY

FRIDAY

SATURDAY

Weekly goals

SUNDAY

MONDAY

TUESDAY

WEDNESDAY

THURSDAY

FRIDAY

SATURDAY

Weekly goals

SUNDAY

MONDAY

TUESDAY

WEDNESDAY

THURSDAY

FRIDAY

SATURDAY

Weekly goals

SUNDAY

MONDAY

TUESDAY

WEDNESDAY

THURSDAY

FRIDAY

SATURDAY

Weekly goals

SUNDAY

MONDAY

TUESDAY

WEDNESDAY

THURSDAY

FRIDAY

SATURDAY

Weekly goals

SUNDAY

MONDAY

TUESDAY

WEDNESDAY

THURSDAY

FRIDAY

SATURDAY

Weekly goals

SUNDAY

MONDAY

TUESDAY

WEDNESDAY

THURSDAY

FRIDAY

SATURDAY

Weekly goals

SUNDAY

MONDAY

TUESDAY

WEDNESDAY

THURSDAY

FRIDAY

SATURDAY

Weekly goals

SUNDAY

MONDAY

TUESDAY

WEDNESDAY

THURSDAY

FRIDAY

SATURDAY

Weekly goals

SUNDAY

MONDAY

TUESDAY

WEDNESDAY

THURSDAY

FRIDAY

SATURDAY

Weekly goals

SUNDAY

MONDAY

TUESDAY

WEDNESDAY

THURSDAY

FRIDAY

SATURDAY

Good work!

If you've completed every page of this workbook, you've done a great job.

I would love to know which exercises you enjoyed most and any other feedback you have.

Please drop me a note at iona@30everafter.com. I'd love to hear from you.

Manufactured by Amazon.ca
Bolton, ON